ALEXANDRIA GREEN

DREAMING AMONGST THE SORROWS AND STARS

DREAMING AMONGST THE
SORROWS AND STARS

I never made this collection alone, I always had help.

From my mother, who told me to keep going and to never give up.

From my eldest sister, who said she was always proud of me.

From my friend, who told me the truth but never told me to stop.

From the love of my life, who said that the only thoughts and feelings that mattered were my own.

CONTENTS

PART I

THE BLACKNESS COMES FIRST.

Trigger warnings:

- Suicide
- Violence
- War
- Emotional distress

GONE

To live by someone else's design is to be chained to a weight that crushes you into dust—particles to float away for eternity—your soul? Dead. An unplanted seed of a beautiful flower—one of a kind—gone. Destroyed beneath the weight of everyone else.

CALAMITY

The tether connecting

my soul to

my body—

snapped!

by a weight

that pulls me

down

down

        down

            down

to the depths of the deep blue sea.

There is no creaking wooden life raft to save me,

no hand outstretched to hold me.

The world of man, pulled away,

eyes rolling in aggravation

The end will push

and pull

   and push

and pull.

I breathe, "Why?"

the dark blue sea replying,

"Why?"

   "Why?"

"Why?"

all

  the

   way

    down

    I

   see

fragments

   of

    my

                              self

swimming in the deep dark sea

my mind

                         scattered—

swimming

                              swimming for air

My body—frozen—

no words, no questions, no

"Why?"

Silent

DREAMS

Another war, more flames

more death; it's all the same...

When will we learn—?

that all the bullets, all the hate...

it takes us in turns,

that we cannot control, in any state,

in any place, in any way

All I dream in my sea of fireflies

surrounded by a world of ink black

is one word:

peace.

I sink in my seat.

My skin tightens with shoulders that shake.

I cry more tears than I can take,

till I can't make anymore—

"peace," I scream.

My actions, my anguish, all because

of these wars.

the ground—filled with oceans of red—shakes

and new rivers are carved brutally

into my face

Why can't my dream come true?

"Let it come true!"

Am I not strong enough

in this storm of blood and bullets?

We're lost in this cloud of pain

It is creating a stain

That we cannot remove

for centuries upon centuries

We cannot redeem our souls

with another spray of blood and an army of bullets

My soul is filled with a troubled pain

am i not strong enough?

I'm trembling with questions that ensue

Torment has consumed my soul

It is in tatters

My last breath of the day

a quiet whispering,

shaking,

Hurting

sigh.

GLASS CEILINGS AND CHANDELIERS

———————————

I hit the glass ceiling, shaking chandeliers from their pristine golden bolts

The ceiling shattered with shouts of ferocity

The rain of glass—hitting me all over my already blemished skin

Beads from diamond chandeliers pierce my heart

fragile as it already was,

unlike the glass ceiling.

In truth, the chandeliers, sparkling with their brilliant diamonds,

was the toughest out of the three of us.

But now I'm sobbing blood—it sparkles like the diamonds tearing at my skin

Now I'm crying out against the pain that perforates my soul

No one hears me—too caught up in the ceiling I broke

or they do hear my near lyrical sobs

but rip the shards of their glass ceiling

tear the chandelier diamonds

out—

of—

me—

to make a stained glass ceiling and new chandeliers of rubies instead

"Because nothing sings better

than color."

And I

am too weak

to argue

to let the sky be seen—unhindered.

UNTITLED I

The constellations of the night, so scattered and shat-
tered

into little jagged glass-like fragments of a bright wailing
sorrow

too far from one another to form

the soul it once was,

to shine like the angelic, comforting beacon it used to be

Lost to the gale after mankind declared their names

and swiftly took from them like well-meaning mission-
aries

All their glow and glory now taken

to the men in their high-seated top hats and gilded
canes of stature

tap, tap, tap

to declare the Lyra—the scene of our great burning fall

that left us hopeless—only to have it

thrown—

into the air, next to the brightly blazing Draco—

the memories that lit us up, into cinders

while we tried sleeping peacefully in our ashen beds

flecks of ash, glinting, floating whimsically, designed after imps and pixies

as mischievous as the moment they breathed themselves into existence

reducing us to bits of dark onyx, as cold as the rocks that created the color

shining with pain

tap, tap, tap

there goes the Cygnus, shot by venomous arrows by hands

that knew

what they were doing

but uncaring, unfeeling

of how they scattered the stars that made up the feathers

those glorious wings, never able to take flight

ever again

never able to feel the purity of flight, of completion

Do they know that Cygnus's stars are flecks of uncolored rubies—blood—

tap, tap, tap—

it never ends—

UNTITLED II

Your Kraken pulled me from my Heavens

to tear my heart open in the burdening cold, black sea

stealing the fire called Soul

in Your name

Decay will set

a struggle—

to breathe in—

this Sea of Thieves

it breeds rivers of Tears, made opaque by the salt—from my wounds

it was not enough for You—it never was—

Your greed was as mountainous as the Goddess Mother of the World and Sky

You had Your Kraken keep me in a sunken cage of cold stalactites

piercing my hollowness that You grew with every word—

tearing my chest into splinters of bone with every—second—You—look—at—me—

until i'm forced onto Death's granite doorstep

but not admitted—

instead, stuck

between

worlds

unable to grace

my Heavens.

UNTITLED III

Crying is an emotional reflex

> —for when the sting of hands and spits of words
> hit you

reeking from the pain of isolation and the stench of
your bedroom

> —as the fear of another missing soul causes terri-
> ble storming tears

Your Heart will never repair the lacerations caused

> —even after centuries pass your soul by

Intuition that has failed you into falling into that trap of
disloyalty

> —will rip you a new one, taking one more piece of
> yourself to the incinerator

Never to be seen Again

> —with the monster you used to call "someone to
> care for, someone to love"

Gasping for air beneath the crippling onslaught of anxiety and depression

—will be the new daily, and bring about a storm of wretched and shivering sobs

THE MEANING IS FOUND

_____

When dawn reveals

the glimmer of rays

I cannot see

See; the way forward

for it is day

Day, an Old English noun:

Light—smothering,

a period of time—

shackled by the light

Haunting for eras,

that is day's meaning.

Haunting my mind,

this single rotation—

My body, stunted

moves of its own accord

I cannot control it—

not until the sun sets

sets of moonlight, peeking through the clouds

clouds of stars blink welcomingly

I will wait hours—

years, almost now

—now the moon shines.

THE NIGHT REMEMBERS

When planning a nightly escape always remember:

1. Knee length boots built for running

You need to run—run—run!

The monsters and their smiles come out

always

at night, when there are shadows quivering and laughing

2. A coat for the cold

because you can't shiver like the shadows,

and you certainly won't be laughing while hiding behind porcelain trees

built to break, and reveal

you and your fear

3. A hair-tie for the hair getting in your face

while you run—

run, remember?

You have to run, to keep your line of sight clear—

like the moon's leopard spots

slinking in and out of the clouds

4. A phone to call your sister or mother

so they can tell you that all your fears, all your imagination spiraling in your head

made from spiderweb silk, delicate yet hard to escape

is just in your head

but valid.

But it's in your head, remember?

There's no need to run.

I AM FROZEN WAITING

I try to get off the large red carousel but it's going too fast

So I wait and sit on the golden ivory bench pulled by stags

and see that the poor black and white horse in front of me has a broken hoof

and it is nowhere to be found, so the horse is left

marred

forever.

Maybe, I think, it was from coming to life, stampeding too fast, trying too hard to get away

away, away, away

from the noise and the screaming—the music that makes ears bleed

It needed to get away, like I *need* to get away

but I'm stuck in an ivory jail cell because the red colors are swirling too fast and if I try to get away I may lose my feet to the spinning and careening,

never able to get up again.

So I sit

and sit...

and sit...

and I feel my hands shaking, gripping my body

I feel my heart thundering too loud

but not louder than the music of the too fast red nightmare I inhabit

So I wait...

and I wait...

and wait...

For it all to stop.

I WAS GONE

I did not wake up today.

Someone Else—Someone Else in my bed—She woke up today.

I was pushed into a shell

hiding

from the pain of Life

while Someone Else pulled me by an invisible taut chain

to make sure I glided along and stayed in my spellbound shell.

The tongue Someone Else took from me was cut

three times

from what crimes I did not know.

I plea in my haze and cry in my sleep

but No One could hear me through the ticking clock of Life—

tick, tick... tick—

Someone Else took me through my days

till I returned, always sitting in my bed, tears flowing down my face

with everything and nothing to say

and Life crowing loudly, "You think you can escape?

My plans are vast and full of winding twists and turns.

There is no escape."

JUST A DREAM

_____

I'm tripping on a branch, falling—falling—

an Alice of Modern Times, wearing ripped jeans and a ribbed crop top—

falling down—down—down—

the rabbit hole!

But I never chased the hare who wore a suit jacket and a golden watch

I chased a yearning that was escaping my body

that tripped on the fire of something unseen

and I fall after it

without desperation, without fear

to the Strange and Bewitching Wonderland.

even though I can't fathom the workings of tea parties and flying card birds

I think of impossibilities every day at a home shaped like a hat and a genius madman who makes me laugh as he serves me giggling cucumber sandwiches.

And as colors of Crimson and Black meet Pearl and Black I sit and try to dissect myself from the misunderstandings

I leapt into—forgetting that there was ever an Overside in the first place.

Because what is life without a little madness and flying fish?

NOTHING IS LEFT

---

tiredness seeps into the very core of my bones

calcium replaced with a yearning darkness that wants to
eat

and eat

and eat

burrowing into every bone until the blood becomes just
as infected

until the soul is

eaten

and eaten

and eaten

only shreds remain

a hollow thing—not a person—stood before a mirror

sighing

looking down at the floor

wondering

how deep would i have to claw before i could even bury the smallest part of my pinkie finger into the sinew of my body

wondering

if instead of a wet coldness wrapping around my insides would there be a blanket of warmth instead

wondering

if my blood would look crimson or if it would be bright yellow with flecks of acid green

wondering and wondering... and wondering

but i was too tired to feed my own curiosity the way the monster fed on me

WE HOLD THE SCYTHE

Do the words "falling meteors" mean anything anymore?

We meteors stay in our towers and cottages in the ivory stonework that makes it up

until the world spins and swirls too much for us to stay

even though we made the world spin this way—far too much

and gravity of all things breaks our orbits so we decide to descend on universes full of laughter and smiles

So we leave our ivory towers and cottages and wreak havoc on the worlds outside

layering it in a twinkling burning frozen-like hellscape, for our anger and fear and bitterness and hatred

so the worlds can be as dark and decayed

And ruined.

like we are.

Damned

like we are.

So the other creatures of furs and scales, of skin, of hides that went about their day stopped

stopped to look at us

us who were descending upon their worlds with unjustified ruin,

swirling above with petrifying fire and an undesirable vengeance

and they trembled

For there was no point

no rhyme or reason, no why

just because, we thought we could, and we harbingers of death did not stop to think

for even a moment.

Not one, not one—even after we destroyed everything good

Everything that was full of life, that had burned with a wonderful warm light

we

destroyed.

BURNING OUT

If you watch a falling star, you shouldn't put it in your pocket, for it did not mean to fall and all it wishes is to return to the world it once knew

not the world it was forced to be in, amidst the cannibals and the soul-sucking monster that claw and tear at every

single

inch

of the star's soul—

a timid, flickering, candle-like delicate thing—

that breaks easily amongst the taloned fingers that wish to take a piece out of the star that is too small to have any pieces taken from its poor soul

and a pocket is too small, too dark for a bright and quivering star full of hopes and dreams of shining silver in the sky of midnight blues

There is one star missing from the sky

except the only ones mourning with an orchestra of wails

are the stars

and the Mother Moon, missing their poor child

While the pockets squeeze and tighten until there was nothing left of the star's soul

since a hand decided to pick it up

to put it in a pocket

and carry it till it died a slow..

torturous...

quiet...

Death.

BY THE OCEAN WITH NO STARS

Hell is cooler than the steel of your gaze

where the life and light fade away to a smokey haze

my eyes glistening with pain, filling with a watery glaze

I couldn't believe that you were my blood; twin to me
you were not

age being the only passable thing between us, like a
sapling to a tree

but the height never frightened the sapling, as it grew,
trying to find the sea

away from the oppressive older tree

for even the sea was warmer and kinder than you.

You, who broke my very soul, like a shrew,

demanding more—more—more—till I broke, and broke, and broke, till I cried like the morning dew

screaming for relief, screaming for solitude, for silence—always

even as I stare at the sky, dark with warm comforting blues, but no stars for stargazing

because you stole all my stars the same day you destroyed my forests by setting them ablaze

now I have nothing left

except the words that leave your mouth, rattling in my head—"blessed"

—and you were in it, unwanted like a crest

As I wear my tears the same

you feel no shame,

Even though you were the one to blame.

LUNA STELLA

The Stars know the Heavens

as I know you, sister

but you, dear sister, will never know me

you who find fault with every facet of my being—yes,
you do

Facets more complex than a crystal, once shattered

now Reborn in a hard, raging red jasper fire—

hours upon hours of tears and screams, trembling, to be
where I am—who I am

like a newborn Constellation, without a name

I will always be unnamed to you

you who cannot be bothered to look Up—no, you can't.

I glimmer in the light, in the Heavens—an open space

where I will create mundane and masterful pieces to shine, and dull, as much as I do

But you will never see it—no, you won't.

you see the world in black and white

I see it in color, with every shade known to the gods

you hear in white, your favorite color

I hear in a kaleidoscope of shapes, colors, and structures

I understand you like the clouds understand the land's need for rain

but you will not, will never understand me, thinking my soul has despicable stains marring it

you don't want to see that I can't be as white as a prison

I must have my facets of color, swirling to make new unknown shades of brilliance

But you will never know it—know me

because you decide to stay far, far away,

refusing to try and look up

to see

My Constellation.

PART II

AND NOW THE LIGHT...

WHAT I SEE IN STARS

———————————————

1. The love of my life, a completion of me, holding me for an eternity

2. A library of my own, to fill my undying thirst for knowledge

3. The wind in my hair as I jump over a fallen log on horseback, the beautiful black and white hindquarters rippling in the air

4. The clean, golden, glimmering sands of Ireland

5. A hall filled with paintings made by van Gogh, yet empty of people so my mind may walk through the poetry of the paintings

6. An ocean waiting for my toes to dip in, waiting for my mind to wander away

7. The need to look up at the stars

and see

SOULFUL

————————————

You may dance your soul out of your

body

on a sun-kissed sandstone pavement

your body having a mind all

on its own

completely—out of your conscious control

You may lose

your mind,

paint something without a name

something made new the moment that last stroke

fell away

from

the

canvas

You may sing something that breaks a soul

in two.

Tears filled with sweet salt

to wet a too dry face that was sobbing

for streaming tears

You may find the ballpoint pen

inescapable—

impossible to

set down

until your soul lets go

of that last word

All of it, the ritual for your universe.

DREAMING WITH STARS

What does it mean—to dream among the shining, dia-
mond-like stars?

In my bones, in the depths of my shadowed and scarred
soul,

I know it means to imagine the most attainable and im-
possible things

Things that you close your eyes for, that you continue to
look for in dreams

things that live in the heavens among the beacons of
hope—they are called stars

Stars, stars, stars—! They are the keys for every keyhole

They are the heartstrings for that pound of flesh in my
chest, the feathers for my wings

since each star is something I've dreamed, the oxygen in
my bloodstream

I need to dream, to keep my hurt soul alive

I need to dream, so that I can *thrive*.

THIS STARRY NIGHT

A swirl of turquoise surrounded by opal lights

begging for my fingers to ruin their lines, their specks of pure white

just so I can feel the kiss of frosted starlight with their black-and-white angel wings, on my fingertips, cool and inviting

Why does the moon resemble a cheshire smile

with lines of charcoal gray marring its gold bar hues

and kitten-like claw marks chiseling away at its body?

And why—why—does it look imperfectly perfect—like home? like fresh bread and melting butter? Why?

And those saintly black-green trees, bending and curving

as if they are ballerinas hitting the sky

all for that one dance move that photographers take photos of and newspapers write articles about

Can I dance with them—bend my body like they do?

Or would I ruin their choreography that they must have spent decades on?

The hills roll and sway, like the mountains ripple, dancing away their centuries of life,

their opaque silicate sparkling beneath the frosted starlight and the cheshire moon

never caring if their dancing shakes the little wooden town nearby

nor should they.

Life is ever-changing, constantly in flux, evolving

till suddenly yesterday is oceans away from today

and tomorrow is light years ahead of today.

And yet, they all—all the iridescent stars, the glowing crescent, the turquoise-navy sky—the rippling hills and white oak town—

are captured

forever

in this one moment

as I stare, enraptured—captive—

dreaming this painting to life.

Dreaming myself into it

for just...

a moment...

and then...

a moment more...

forever.

THE DARK GIFT

The blackness of twilight is not something scary and full of terror.

It is a calming love of a blanket on a cold night

next to the fireplace that pops and cracks from the wood

releasing the sweet delightful scent that has no name except comfort.

You could curl up with the twilight for hours and hours, losing all sense of time like a seafarer.

Time has no meaning beneath the twilight stars who blink so bright

It's a sweet and pure sense of godlike light—better than angels, better than sainthood

There is nothing of pain and regret, there is nothing of discomfort.

The blanket will never fray, never lose its bold dark inky color

The fireplace will continue to crackle and pop like the sweet music of a symphony

Time will continue to have no meaning, becoming less and less than a concept

And the serenity will never leave...

Until sunrise.

SNOW DANCES WHILE I FALL

———————————

I jumped at the sight of the snow that shimmied through the air

It was a different scene that pushed me to the edge, weightless

I flew through the air to catch a beautiful silvery ice blue snowflake

its shimmer was pure starlight woven with the light of first day

Selene and Helios working as one, two sides, one purpose: beauty beyond all compare

a beauty that not even Eris could argue against

a beauty that even Aphrodite stood to watch, for hours... for days, if she could.

But that beauty evaded me, made me break my flight amongst the clouds

made me fall to earth, disappointment lining my eyes

a grim line beneath my nose and sadness filling the space on my face

So I waited

and waited, for the day

for winter and snow

ice and flurries

of sunlight mixed with the light of the stars.

I needed snowflakes, delicate and pure with their rainbow fractal pieces

to show me the beauty of the world, when most places refuse to show even a single stream of light

The day came when they arrived, dancing in the wind like ballerinas in Swan Lake

so I reached into the heavens as I did last year, reaching higher and faster—harder—so that I could catch

a swirling, twirling, pirouetting pearly blue snowflake

its luminescence the evidence of Selene and Helios's tender care

Stunning and shining—

I reached—

Failed—

Started falling from my flight—

Reached again, more—

If I could not have this beautiful spinning, gliding snowflake of opalescent sunlight and pure sky blue starlight

I would have to wait

till next year

And wait

and wait...

and...

wait.

A SECOND THOUGHT ON THE WIND

———————————

I thought it was gone

like ash in the wind after a fire

but little did I know it would stay

in the air, as a musky salted aroma

perforating my mind

collecting itself on my skin

catching on the tendrils of my hair

telling me in the sweetest voice

that I was not done

that it was not over

that there *was* more

and I only needed to stop

to close my eyes

and feel it.

QUEEN OF DARKNESS AND LIFE

She came to like a whisper on the wind, every time,

speaking softly like a twinkle of stars and faeries wings, every time

and her clothes were built and woven our of pure sun-light—always luxurious—showing her womanly curves

golden skin off-set by the shimmering sunset red dress, always

With care to hold me like a mother would to her long lost daughter, never,

forgetting to wear her crown that sparkled like obsidian spikes and crystallized jade leaves, never

letting it come off her head, even in the home of her own goddess mother, forever,

showing me how much I have grown with her steady cal-loused hands guiding my shaking one;

showing me how much we were the same in one sense and another, smiling at me with the warmth of a hearth, proud, forever.

Forever, her daughter in the way that the heavens gave birth to the moon and stars,

Forever.

A SPARK

_____

Designed to create something new

to weave together the threads of emotions and thoughts

to burrow into the soul of a body

so that a gleaming smile of joy is born

amid a dark and shadowed day.

Born to step on the stones of a decayed and dying bridge

only instead of walking away

it walks across, almost floating in the air

and once it finishes its journey it looks back

and sees

something old and something new

reborn with the sweat and desire to be

finished.

but one thing is as clear as a yellow-peridot sun in a topaz sky

it was made to be used

to be coveted

to never be disregarded or ignored

because something as intangible and as powerful as a Spark

can be as rare as a bloodless diamond.

STEPPING STONES OF STARS

I leapt from solid ground, green and lush with life, silky
to my curling toes

and land on a stone that wobbles, almost causing my fall

except I crouched and held my ground, clinging, unwill-
ing to leave just yet.

I noticed the smoothness, the sparkling radiance that
emitted from the surface of the stone

and thought that maybe this was my home

but the stone was sinking, unwilling to have me stay

so I forced my feet into the air

to leap

to another stone that had swirls of glowing opal light

a light the color of a swan's feather, I mused

and a luminosity as soft as one, as warm as one

except it too did not want me

even though I had felt that this was my home, that I could be happy here

Instead I leapt again, to another stone that felt like a velvet blanket in a chilled night,

soothing and warm, with a feeling of contentment blooming deep inside my core

only that stone, too, did not want me

and lest I find my knees becoming as wet as my ankles in that aqua blue water

I had to leap.

I found myself one stone away from the other side

A smile burst onto my face as my feet landed on that next stone—the last stone

with a phosphorous cadence like a star's—so bright and full—

a cataclysm of euphoria seeping into my very veins, making them glow an unearthly shade

except the stone didn't want me either—this last one

so I forced myself to leap

and hit the other side of the river.

And I laughed, a twinkle, rippling throughout the air

and I continued to produce that melody

because that light, that warmth, that euphoria *burning in me* meant

that I found home

by never stopping,

by leaping and leaping and leaping

By becoming

a Star.

IT IS ENDLESS

———————————

At night I stargaze, because within each star I see

countless possibilities

a new beginning to each story

a new ending to each life

So I sip my strawberry tea

and look into the. stars to watch each and every possi-
bility

And in a fractal blue star I see a love born and grown
throughout lifetimes

a love to put fated mates and star-crossed lovers to
shame.

Within a green star so small one must squint to see

there lies a cottage by the seaside, made with pinewood
and white mortar

glimmering with happiness erupting with laughter

and I cannot help the smile spreading across my face

while I lift my steaming cup of tea

patterned in golden swirls erupting against jade.

The way I devour the pinkish liquid is the same way

I devour those possibilities.

Sea after sea

those possibilities light a fire in my heart

to show me that there is more to life

than one thinks.

There is a picnic by the stone garden quay

with a family who smiles while enjoying each other's bright companionship

inside the radiance of a twinkling amber star

that stares at me from its seat next to the blue sister star.

The more I watch the more time is spent.

stargazing in my wicker lounge chair, content to watch lives be born and turn the clock they hold

until my jade and gold cup turns cold and empty

telling me, I must go inside, and wait for the new stars of tomorrow.

THE AUTHOR

My vision blurs

One more word

Another?

My handwriting is that of a drunken person

letters I do not recognize as my own.

Exhaustion

too many late nights cramming

Book

after

Book

after

Book—

Inked word

after

Inked word—

My thirst dries my scaly tongue

Thick, terrible. Distracting.

One more word.

My legs are too tired to make the journey up eleven stairs

so, defeated, they stay in place so that I may write

One more word.

Except the word that comes to mind is sleep

Sleep.

Sleep.

One foot

after

the other

after

the other

to my villainous velvet bed

to sleep.

Sleep so that I have a day of unblurred words and recognizable lettering

until my soul becomes weary once more, demand-
ing *only*

One more word

before

Sleep.

A RARE FORM OF LIGHTNING

———————————

What lies within a smile are the sparks of lightning

crystallized onto bone, canvassed by flesh

and draped in a glow that encompasses every inch of skin.

What creates the sparks of lightning is a collision of euphoria

and harmony—set into the body like a sword in a crystal stone—

too difficult for just anyone to remove

and even more impossible to replicate.

A smile is a rarity—even Merlin and Morgana agree, together, as the Dark and Light do

It is something that should be cherished

memorized in memory

like the dying breath of a dragon,

watched from beginning to end—not squandered for even a moment.

Those who watch the white-blue lightning become wreathed in its hazy warmth

tingling with the same harmony

that crashes into an ethereal bliss

creating even more—crystallized lightning.

BREAK DOWN, BREAK THROUGH, BREAK FREE

We skipped all the tolls

so we could shock both our souls

with the greedy hands we possess

and the signs that were musically stressed.

Our bodies collided, sparks of electricity hitting air without a single lull

a passion as raw and quaking as the cracking destruction of a mountain—

Colors in shades of vibrant midnight blue collided—

with shades of viciously vicarious rouge—

An explosion of lavender haze leveled our world

creating a plane of fantastical realities

And then you leveled *my* world—my skin

with imprints of your love—

Teeth biting soft and bruised and blushed skin.

There are no doves

in our world,

since we don't care to dance in the skies

Rather, we want to slam our sweat glistening bodies onto the fiery ground of Hell

where inhibitions are shattered by the sounds of ecstasy

and lessons, rules, societal graces—all the lies—

are thrown to the fire, to drown in it, bursting sponta- neously—screaming, never to tell all the lies

ever again.

For every hiss of pleasure, every cry of breathtaking re- lease, we gain

a truth—of the world, of each other, of ourselves

that no society can give us

for lust—lust for each other, for pleasure, reaching past Jupiter—

is wonderfully unruly, taboo, breaking all the rules

as beautiful and as sweet to the tongue as Juniper

As dazzling, as clear-cut, and as colorful as all the world's jewels.

Our world of undignified bodies moving like water

amid our pleasure-filled crass cursing

heady moans—

There is nothing more naturally Holy.

PART III

**SOMETIMES, THE LIGHT CANNOT EVADE
THE BLACKNESS...**

DREAMING IN THE DEPTHS OF MY MIND

———————————

It's nothingness—a blackness, soothing

like silk, wrapping my mind as if it were a baby to be swaddled

A coldness seeps into the lines of my brain

rivers frozen solid, frosty with the weight of tainted memories

a pain to speed my heart faster than the speed of sound

a whimpering to cause the air to ripple—

a stone dropped in a pond

rippling—

The hands wrap around me, as they wrap around my mind,

are tender and as warm as clouds, pulling me to see a face of love

Warm chocolate eyes, sparkling with sea salt—

A rosy blush, blooming like carnations and lilies

in a field filled with a tenor laughter

that washes away the shadowy pain like a cleansing rainfall filled with pure light

light—

Stormy eyes see a swirl of a ceiling fan

Swish, swish, swish—

Awakened from a torrent of dreams

BENEATH THE DREAMS, ALWAYS

Beyond the rays of moonlight is a world of dreams

Pure kingdoms filled with magick that twinkles in the air

swirling and caressing the very fabric of reality, twisting it into something

New

Dragons who flash through the clouds and roar with a might fury

a roar that shakes the very air—

Ferociously

Faeries with wings of powdery vines twisting to fly, giggle mischievously

causing chaos to stir in the very souls of those they cross—

Fiends

Merfolk gather their shells and pearls to create the most beautiful crowns and rings

to create crests of light, to streak throughout the waters as they sing

Melodically

Each one is a dream to fog the air around the violent and thrashing nightmares

Of enchantresses creating spells to enslave mankind

with their rich and dark beauty, their cavernous power—

Dangerous

The slithering basilisks with eyes of pure venom and acid in their fangs

dripping, sizzling, burning the ground into nothingness, into

Dust

Terrifying tempests of stcrm spirits, writhing and screaming in the air

vengeance marking their eyes like arrows hungry for targets, starving,

Wanting

More wanting than even the undead spirits longing for rest amongst the whistles of trees and the chaotic ripples of lakes

Mirrors stared at them and their eyes grew horrified at the ragged, skeletal, *hollow* look of themselves—their mouths opened...

Screaming

Nightmares become the obsidian hell with layers of fire and endless forests for the wandering—

The fog that revealed the kingdom of fire and forests returns, shading the pain and fear

making way for the dreams clothed in twinkling and shining gold—

Paradise.

Until the hellscape returns once more.

The cycle is renewed.

UNABLE TO REACH

There is a chasm as deep, as full as the center of the earth, burrowing into every part of my heart

corrupting every thread of my soul with a corrosive red that seeps like acid into the gold twinkling silver of my soul

A soul that yearns to mimic a mockingbird and speak the truth to the world verse after verse

A soul that yearns to see shelves filled with the words that have been written by my cracked and calloused hands

A soul that yearns to be twinned with another soul that knows every part, every dark and broken crevice of my soul

filling one another with a love so pure...so light... so good, and imperfectly perfect

that the burrowing, burning corrosion, the suffering the trickling tears that makes rivers seem small

ceases.

WAYS TO FIND STARS

Amidst the dreams that perforate even your every day to keep away the monsters of thievery at bay who just take—take—take—never stopping

In the oceans where kelp beds and seaweed forests sway in the turquoise-green waters, drowning out the sounds of screaming and yelling—for more, for something new, for a future that won't seem to come

In the fields where the grass whispers delights to waiting ears and the only sounds heard are all the ways the jade blades will tickle ankles and calves, and not say a word about all the ways women are losing their voices

Where the sounds of squirrels and rabbits run through the evergreen forests, pushing into trees and burrowing into dens—to hide from the man-wolves—saying that tomorrow maybe better, that they may be safe

In the clouds amongst the birds who fly free and un-bridled, hollering with joy—without a care in there world—without anyone to say the words, "Stay out of the clouds, out of the sky—you should not fly." Which is the same as saying, "Do not breathe," and the same as locking souls in small metal caskets six feet under the ground with no light and no sky

Inside the glistening caverns that create symphonies that change at every turn of the head—willing the tears of women and children who wish to escape from this world to be Silent—willing a peace to hatch and grow in this mad, mad world

inside the small spaces between pain and cruelty, stars can be found, can be held and caressed—inside moments of sleep, of exploration, limitless imagination—

stars can be found.

THE GODDESS VENUS

She was in my already full mind, maddening me

nonstop

Her visage haunted the dark and shadowed hallways I
walked

every damn day—

Her soul carefully collected itself to careen my
thoughts—

every fucking second.

She wanted the canvas to be filled with the soulful blue
of Her skin,

She wanted Her fiery golden eyes to never be forgotten

for She was not just Love,

She was Retribution too.

THE FLAMES IGNITED

Its tendrils of gauzy clouds

and amber whips

wove themselves together, careful not to disturb

the stars and moons that etched themselves into

the russet colored sky.

If one were to stretch out a hand to touch them

they would find they were met

with hisses and red ruby scratches

of violent rage

and vengeful retribution.

Because sometimes the most beautiful creations on
earth—

the most heavenly piece of artifice to grace the ether of
the universe

should not be touched

but instead

only seen.

REASONS TO LOVE THE NIGHT

_____

I look up instead of down

>   because looking down on Father Earth only brings
>   sorrow
>
>   only brings pain with its twisting vines to entan-
>   gle me.
>
>   Father Earth never cared to look at me
>
>   or look up at what I had done
>
>   and Father Earth only ever taught me to look
>   down
>
>   and hold in my tears, breathing so quietly I may as
>   well be in a wooden chestnut casket
>
>   so when I look at Mother Night I know to look up
>
>   and I smile
>
>   for the loving that She wreaths me in

I see stars instead of darkness

> since the Mother of Night always gives me Her brightest stars each night

> and not the darkness of a cold face with no love

> no recognition, Father Earth, that I am yours.

> That merciless silence, that icy shadow—one can never see it in Mother Night

> only from you, Father Earth, in the crevices of the lines of your unforgettable face.

I was given a new name that sparked a starlight world inside my veins

> and not a sickening dissociation of asking myself, "Who am I—if not

> your daughter, Father Earth?"

> Never have I heard the words "beloved" or "daughter" escape the Earth's chaste lips

> only in the gleam of the moon and the shining stars of Mother Night

> She. calls me wonderful daughter, loving daughter, beautiful daughter

> and yet all pale in comparison to the new name She gifted me one midnight night

It pulled asunder the weeds and cracked earth left
behind by the father who was not my father

New life was grown from the cold ashes left behind

    by Father Earth

    with the tender care and warm love from Mother
    Night's watchful gaze

    never leaving me even as the Sun rises

    never leaving me

    as the earth did.

IT'S ALIVE

Beneath the surface of each star there beats a dream

that yearns to be set free

by a fiery explosion of a soul

destined for more than what they think

The confines of thoughts and doubts become an awful regime

wherein the poor dream must wait

for months or years

till the dystopia crumbles into nothing but memory

The explosion of soul will then blaze bright, burning away at the lifeless colors of gray and black to create a new color scheme

filling atmosphere after atmosphere in a maze of wonder

that makes even the Seven Deadly Sins bend their knees with grace

And so in the end, there is a creation of a utopia.

The dystopian regime has fallen, making way for the savior of a soul:

A Dream.

THE SPIRIT OF TAURUS

I have hooves that cause earthquakes of the same magnitude that is given to the Minotaur

I have horns that will never break and only ruin those who dare stand in my way

I have a hide that cannot be pierced, even by godly means

I have a spirit so fiery, so fearsome, that it puts Pompeii to shame

I am a wild beast who stands on two feet

I am a terrible storm that will ruin my enemies

I am a rock, standing tall, never wavering, never breaking

I am the force that keeps my loved ones steady and safe

I am unstoppable

I dare someone to *try* and stop me

from anything.

ABOUT THE AUTHOR

Alexandria Green graduated with honors from Illinois Wesleyan University in 2025 with a degree in creative writing and a minor in journalism and media. All her life she has wanted to publish her poetry and prose, and her short stories and novels. She made stories as a little girl and kept them in a toy chest, constantly changing them after writing them, convinced they weren't ready to be seen. Despite loving to write, Alexandria didn't enjoy reading until she read Percy Jackson by Rick Riordan for the first time. After that it was hard to keep a book out of her hand.

She has always wanted to share her ideas and creativity, showing the world that they aren't alone. When she is not reading or writing (and editing), she is most likely playing video games, binging Supernatural or a DC show, or generally being a chaotic coffee gremlin. Alexandria typically hangs out in a coffee shop, a library or bookstore, or in the basement of her home—aka her Batcave. Her favorite author *currently* is Sarah J. Maas and her favorite poet will always be Emily Dickinson.

Her second poetry collection *Loving Across Galaxies* can be found on Barnes & Noble, Amazon, or the Bookshop.

For more information go to Instagram and view her account, @alexthereaderwriter, or visit her website alexthereaderwriter.wordpress.com.

www.ingramcontent.com/pod-product-compliance
Lightning Source LLC
Chambersburg PA
CBHW070347130626
46556CB00007B/3062